SUMMARY & ANALYSIS

OF

LEADERSHIP

IN TURBULENT TIMES

★ ★ ★ ★ ★ ★ ★ ★ ★ ★ ★ ★ ★ ★

A GUIDE TO THE BOOK
BY DORIS KEARNS GOODWIN

BY *ZIP*READS

NOTE: This book is a summary and analysis and is meant as a companion to, not a replacement for, the original book.

Please follow this link to purchase a copy of the original book: https://amzn.to/2Q66mg0

TABLE OF CONTENTS

SYNOPSIS

Leadership: In Turbulent Times is the detailed recounting of the life, struggle, and leadership of three of the greatest American presidents and one whose legacy was left divided. Doris Kearns Goodwin follows the lives of Abraham Lincoln, Theodore Roosevelt, Franklin Roosevelt, and Lyndon Johnson from their youths through their deaths. She addresses the adversity they each faced that helped them transform into the great leaders they became, and she provides detailed examples of the styles of leadership they each possessed.

The book is divided into four sections, with the first covering the early years of each future president. The second section focuses on the hardships they had to overcome that led to their capacity for greatness, and then covers their actions as president as concrete examples of the leaders they became. In her epilogue, she discusses the death of each of the four men, two of whom died in office, and the men they had grown to be, or the men they still wished they could have been.

The book is an exhaustive examination of what makes a great leader, how powerful decisions are made, how tragedy can make or break a man, and how every man, no matter how great, is forced to live with the decisions he has made.

PART I: AMBITION AND THE RECOGNITION OF LEADERSHIP

ABRAHAM LINCOLN: A MAN BORN TO LEAD

Though incredibly poor and the child of an illiterate farmer, Lincoln was a gifted and determined student who excelled in every class. He was as domineering physically as he was gregarious—he loved to entertain people as a child and his personality was larger than life.

After he was taken out of school to work on the farm, Lincoln took it upon himself to continue his education. He was a voracious reader and absorbed every story, every book he could get his hands on when he wasn't busy plowing the fields for his father.

As soon as he was 21, he left his father's fields to strike out on his own, getting a job as a clerk at the general store in the town of New Salem. The people of New Salem immediately fell in love with Abraham, always kind, funny, eager to learn, willing to help a stranger, and never expecting anything in return. The townspeople liked him so much, they convinced him to run for state legislature shortly after he moved to town.

His original platform included the creation of a national bank, protective tariffs, governmental support for internal improvements, and an expanded public education system.

Abraham displayed early on in his life a willingness to acknowledge errors and to learn from his mistakes. Though he lost his first campaign, he was appointed deputy surveyor for Sangamon County, allowing him to travel between towns. His reputation as a storyteller preceded him and people came to the town centers just to hear him speak. In his second attempt at running for state legislature, he easily won.

When he arrived, however, he remained quiet. He was busy absorbing and learning, aware that he didn't know enough about how things worked to take action.

"A finely developed sense of timing—knowing when to wait and when to act—would remain in Lincoln's repertoire of leadership skills the rest of his life" (Goodwin, p. 14).

When Lincoln saw how much studying law would benefit his career as a legislator, he taught himself that as well by reading borrowed law books alone at night.

In the legislature's second session, he no longer sat on the sidelines. His broad understanding of legal terminology and parliamentary procedure and his fine penmanship were invaluable in drafting legislation. Beyond those hard skills, however, was his talent for oration and an intuition for the feelings and inclinations of politicians on both sides of the aisle. He was elected by the Whig caucus as their minority leader.

At the age of twenty-six, Lincoln was one of only six out of seventy-seven legislators to vote against codifying slavery in the state constitution saying, "if slavery is not wrong, nothing is wrong" (p. 17). But his main goal at the time was to bring infrastructure spending and education to small rural areas in the state, not to fight slavery. In just a few years as a legislator, Lincoln had become a respected leader, and a champion of equality, liberty, and opportunity.

THEODORE ROOSEVELT: A MAN WHO OVERCAME

Where Lincoln wrote a two-thousand-word manifesto proclaiming his desire to run for office and detailing his platform, Theodore "Teedie" Roosevelt wrote just thirty-three words confirming his desire to run. Politics had changed significantly in the half-century since Lincoln ran; campaigning no longer happened through casual conversation in the general store. Roosevelt was nominated by one of the party bosses and ran mostly on the name of his father, a well-known and well-loved philanthropist in New York. Local politics at the time was more of a boys' club that met in smoke-filled rooms and required a recommendation by other members to join than a grassroots operation. Where Lincoln was poor, Roosevelt was privileged. Where Lincoln was gregarious with a strong constitution, Roosevelt was timid as a child and plagued by asthma. Where Lincoln educated himself against his father's wishes, Roosevelt was endlessly encouraged.

Roosevelt believed both in innate genius and hard work, but thought himself more blessed with the latter than the former. He read voraciously throughout his life, and his wealth meant, unlike Lincoln, he had easy access to any book he might want. He believed that in order to lead, one must understand human nature, and the best way to do that was "by the great imaginative writers, whether of prose or poetry."

At Harvard, Theodore was beyond studious. He was socially awkward and often elitist, though had overcome his asthma to participate in sports from rowing to wrestling to tennis. He started myriad clubs and continued his collecting of birds and insects. He was always a naturalist at heart, and he seemed not to care what anyone thought of him.

The hardest event of Teedie's young life was the death of his father at age forty-six. Theodore Roosevelt, Sr. was heavily involved in politics and once told Teedie, "I fear for your future. We cannot stand so corrupt a government for any length of time" after losing out on a prestigious nomination to to the corrupt "machine politicians."

While his father's death was painful, it also motivated him to do better, to be better. Teedie transformed himself from an elitist who turned his nose up at lower classes to a universally sociable person who acted without condescension. He moved away from a career in sciences, not wanting to spend his life looking at a microscope, but still clung to his passions as a naturalist. He thought about taking on philanthropy or law, though he didn't care for either. Through his outreach across class lines he realized that "no man is superior, unless it was by merit, and no man is inferior, unless by his demerit" (p. 32). He began getting involved with working-class Irish and German immigrants who were able to see past his quite dandy appearance for the good-natured and forthright person he was. In these circles is where he met the local boss Joe Murray who nominated him for office.

He readily won by refusing to pander to anyone's demands and proclaiming himself untouched by the political machine. Unlike Lincoln's quiet first term, Teedie was involved, making a name for himself as a highly vocal opponent of corruption. He believed himself the champion of good against evil, though his rise to political stardom quickly went to his head. His consistent outbursts against Democrats became too much, too aggressive, and he lost support from even Republicans in his policy initiatives. Understanding this loss, luckily, led him to realize the importance of cooperation and the truly nuanced nature of morality and politics.

In his early years, his laissez-faire economic policy to oppose minimum wage and limit working hours was softened by a sense of empathy for the conditions of the working class. The more he exposed himself to these people with whom he had had no interaction, the more he understood the harm in the harsh divisions between social classes. By his third term in the assembly, he was committed to overcoming divisive politics to pass real reform in New York City.

FRANKLIN ROOSEVELT: A LATE BLOOMER

In contrast to Abraham and Theodore, Franklin did not project leadership qualities early in life. He was neither particularly strong, ambitious, driven, nor intelligent. He followed a traditional career path into a Wall Street law firm where he also failed to impressive with his work ethic or accomplishment. At twenty-eight, where Abraham and Theodore had already made their mark on politics and solidified themselves as leaders, Franklin had done nothing of note. Despite this, he received an offer from the party bosses to run for a safe Democratic seat in the State Assembly of New York, more for the Roosevelt name than for him personally. He jumped at the chance.

Franklin turned out to be a natural to politics. He was a skilled listener, full of warmth and charisma to whom people naturally gravitated. His "self-assured, congenial, optimistic temperament" would be talked about by generations of historians as the "keystone to his leadership success" (Goodwin, p. 43).

By all accounts, Franklin had a near perfect childhood. His parents were in a loving marriage; he was an only child who was sheltered from any ugliness or conflict while living on a wealthy country estate. He was universally described as a bright and happy child. When his father suffered a debilitating heart attack when Franklin was just eight, he became a sort of placator and protector, aiming always to please. With fewer outdoor activities, he retreated into stamp collecting, which would remain his mental respite throughout his life, even during his presidency.

Unlike both Lincoln and Theodore Roosevelt, Franklin wasn't an exemplary student in the traditional sense. He didn't pore over prose or poetry, but he possessed a curiosity and intelligence that spanned subjects, ever-inspired by the history behind a particular stamp or the people of that country.

When he was sent to Groton boy's school at the age of twelve, Franklin had yet to interact with other boys his age and found himself struggling to make friends with his prim, buttoned-up demeanor that adults so adored. By the time he entered Harvard after his father's death, he was struggling to assert his independence from his now lonely mother. His fifth cousin, Theodore Roosevelt, had just become president of the United States. At school, Franklin rose in the ranks of the *Harvard Crimson* until finally becoming editor his senior year. He was only just beginning to come into himself.

The ability to make decisions without hesitating or looking back—one of his greatest leadership qualities—was first exhibited in his marriage to his cousin Eleanor. Knowing his mother would be heartbroken, he did not leave the issue up for discussion instead presenting it in a final, decisive manner. Marrying Eleanor—a socially-conscious woman who shunned the debutante lifestyle—awakened something in Franklin who realized he wanted to do good as well, to give back.

The assembly seat promised to Franklin by Murray, however, was taken away when the incumbent decided to stay. Franklin decided instead to run for a much more prestigious Senate seat against a firmly entrenched Republican. His first campaign in 1910 marked the largest margin of victory by any Democratic candidate in New York.

Once in the Senate, Franklin faced the same trajectory as his older cousin: rising quickly to greatness fighting against the corruption of the Tammany machine, but being defeated by his own ego and inability to compromise. Luckily, as with his cousin, the ordeals in the Senate taught him the power of bridging factions and striking bargains. When Woodrow Wilson came into office, having seen Franklin's work against Tammany, he quickly appointed the young Roosevelt to assistant secretary of the navy—a post that Franklin had personally coveted and one in which Theodore had also served. Franklin already had his eyes on the presidency, and this was the very path he predicted it would take.

Because Franklin's intelligence was not in rote memorization or book smarts, but rather in outside-the-box thinking and abstract connection, it wasn't until his post in the navy that Franklin's true intelligence—his ability to quickly grasp the completeness of a situation—came to be seen. In the years before the first world war, Franklin had the foresight to bolster the strength and readiness of the naval forces. He had a reputation for finding a way to get things done when everyone said it was impossible. He was willing to put himself on the line to do it, and he was ready to accept responsibility for failure and move on to the next idea if his plans didn't work. Goodwin goes into great detail describing specific conversations he had during his time as assistant secretary of the navy demonstrating his prowess, foresight, and unique ability to move a slow bureaucracy forward.

Once the Allied Forces won the war, Franklin's stint in the navy was done, but he was quickly made the vice-presidential nominee in 1920, solidifying his place as a future potential president. Though the Democratic ticket was sure to lose after eight years in power and a country weary of progressive reform—and it did—the campaign displayed yet another great leadership quality in Franklin: his ability to put together a loyal and committed team. That team would remain by him for years to come and one member, Louis Howe, would remain his most trusted advisor until his death.

LYNDON JOHNSON: A TIRELESS WORKER

Lyndon Johnson's father, Sam Johnson, was a popular politician in the Texas state legislature who often took Lyndon along as he campaigned across the Texas countryside. Both men were likable and were known to strike up conversations with anyone they met. Lyndon's love of visiting the statehouse and hitting the campaign trail with his father, however, could have been attributed to how difficult things often were at home. In contrast to Franklin Roosevelt's perfection of a childhood, Lyndon's mother was deeply unhappy after marrying his father, relegated to fetching water and scrubbing floors despite being a well-bred woman who had attended Baylor University and had dreams of becoming a writer.

Lyndon himself was his mother's sole joy, even after bearing four more children, but her affections were as overflowing when she was pleased as they were icy when she was crossed. This same demeanor would make its mark on Lyndon himself who would "blanket someone with generosity, care, and affection, but in recompense, expect total loyalty and sterling achievement" (Goodwin, p. 72). If that person failed to live up to his standards, they would be on the receiving end of what became known as the Johnson "freeze-out."

At the Southwest Texas State Teachers College, Lyndon weaseled his way into a position in the university president's office through first becoming a janitor before eventually being promoted to the president's errand boy and messenger. Due to his intimate knowledge of politics given him by his father, Lyndon was brought to committee hearings and even began to work up reports. Over time, Lyndon took over many more tasks for President Evans, though most of his fellow students saw him as an ingratiating brown-noser.

His first true position of leadership was as principal of a small Mexican-American elementary school in Texas. It was here he had the chance to exude the leadership qualities he had so long been cultivating. His experience at the impoverished school in Cotulla, Texas would forever change his views on leadership, empathy, and generosity.

"His unflagging energy, his ferocious ambition, and his compulsive drive to organize were now linked to something larger than himself" (Goodwin, p. 76).

Like Abraham, Theodore, and Franklin, Lyndon also shared a fondness and a gift for storytelling. Lyndon was enamored with the heroic cowboy tales of his granddad, Theodore with the rugged life of wilderness men. Only Lincoln—who toiled poor on the farms and worked to escape that life—refrained from glorifying the past in the stories he told.

Despite his love of politics and penchant for storytelling from a very young age, Lyndon's political start was accidental at best. After jumping up for an impromptu speech in favor of a candidate at a town picnic in 1930, he caught the notice of Welly Hopkins, a man about to run for the State Senate. After helping Welly campaign (and securing his victory), Welly recommended Lyndon as legislative secretary to a congressman. Immediately upon arriving in Washington, Lyndon vowed to become a congressman himself.

As Congressman Richard Kleberg's chief of staff, Johnson was an endless fount of energy and dedication. He hired a staff and worked ceaselessly, expecting them to do exactly the same, and always to perfection. He was a man without pastimes who spent every waking moment working politics, reading politics, or talking about politics if he could.

This single-minded determination was applied equally in his courtship of Lady Bird Taylor, to whom he proposed on the second date and married that same day. Lady Bird—ever the balancing wheel to Lyndon's harried impatience—was likely an integral part of his rise in politics as her hospitality led to the close friendship of Lyndon and Congressman Sam Rayburn.

When Franklin Roosevelt created the National Youth Administration in 1935, Lyndon asked Sam to recommend him for the state director of the program in Texas. Despite Lyndon being only twenty-six and having no relevant experience, Roosevelt gave him the job. Johnson's unmatched ability to organize and relentless work ethic were up to the task.

But, as the author points out, he was no easy man to work with. Like his mother, he would oscillate between showering you with praise and berating you for failure. He pitted workers against one another, usually a terrible leadership style. But the Texas NYA succeeded because his staff believed they were working towards something valuable for a person they believed would take them to great things.

In 1937, less than two years after being appointed to the NYA, the death of a congressman meant an opening in Lyndon's district. He knew instantly he had to run, and he did so as a complete unknown against eight more experienced opponents. He worked harder, longer, and smarter than all of them and won by more than 3,000 votes.

When Lyndon entered congress, President Roosevelt met him and was immediately taken with his vigor and drive. Roosevelt would be one of many paternal mentors who guided Lyndon's life, his father and Sam Rayburn included. In his first years in Washington, Lyndon was a dynamo, working to electrify rural Texas and get housing projects built in Austin, among other significant accomplishments. But mostly, his first term in congress was dominated by his reputation as a non-stop go-getter who "was so on his toes, and so active, and so overwhelming."

PART II: ADVERSITY AND GROWTH

When some people are faced with great adversity in their lives, it destroys them. Others are set back considerably and never truly recover. But for these four great men, Goodwin explores how the adversity they faced shaped them; how they not only overcame it but were the better for it.

ABRAHAM LINCOLN

Key Takeaway: In 1840, Lincoln fell into a great depression.

In the throes of a recession, Lincoln's great plans to bring economic development to rural Illinois literally and figuratively crumbled. The projects were halted, and the state fell deeply into debt for all the unfinished construction. As land value plummeted and people lost their homes, Lincoln resigned from his place on the legislature in shame and returned home. In addition to his professional failure, he also decided to back out of his engagement to Mary Todd due to her unpredictable nature as well as to his own financial instability. He was then faced with the shame of ruining her socially and of breaking his own word. Lincoln became both despondent and suicidal for months, finally proclaiming:

"Whether I shall ever be better I can not tell; I awfully forebode I shall not. To remain as I am is impossible; I must die or be better, it appears to me" (p. 100).

After realizing he must indeed "die or be better," he committed himself to the latter. Forming a partnership with Steven Logan, a prominent lawyer in the county, Lincoln finally found financial stability and began to exit his depression. He reentered his engagement with Mary Todd and vowed himself to be a patient, involved husband and father.

Key Takeaway: After another stint in politics, Lincoln reentered law with a newfound vigor for life.

After serving two years in Congress with the hopes of being appointed to Zachary Taylor's administration, Lincoln came home a self-perceived failure once again, throwing himself into his legal practice and into his studies. During this intense period, he consumed as much knowledge as possible, studying from early in the morning until late at night and practicing law during the day. He absorbed every subject he could from Euclidian math to philosophy and astronomy. He emerged from this crucible of dedication and personal growth a wholly new man by all personal accounts of those who knew him.

As the United States expanded, and slavery became a more prominent issue with new states joining the nation, Lincoln became an eminent voice against slavery's expansion, earning himself the moniker "The Great Pacificator" for his role in the Missouri Compromise in 1850. When that ended with the controversial Kansas-Nebraska Act, Lincoln found it his personal mission to advocate against it. In a famed seven-hour debate with Steven Douglas, Lincoln delivered a speech that marked the beginning of the man he would be known as in the annals of history.

The power of his speech lay not just in his storytelling, which he always possessed, but in his newly honed powers of language, logic, and conviction. He unfolded narratives, provided direction, and connected directly to the people. The depth of his conviction led to their conviction. As the essayist Walter Benjamin wrote, "Counsel woven into the fabric of real life is wisdom."

Key Takeaway: Hard work, humility, and leadership led to Lincoln's nomination for president.

Before his own ambitions for Senate, Lincoln was a champion of the newly formed Republican party—a coalition of factions from different parties who left in opposition to the Nebraska bill. The antislavery movement was now paramount to everything for Lincoln, and he twice sacrificed his own chance at a Senate seat lest the tenuous new party divide against itself and be conquered. This personal sacrifice for the good of the party and the movement no doubt played a part in the support he garnered for his presidential nomination, as did his historic speeches in the famed Lincoln-Douglas debates during his race for the Senate. Lincoln may have won the debates and gained national notoriety, but Stephen Douglas won the U.S. Senate seat in 1858.

When Lincoln quietly began his bid for president in 1860, he was still the least well-known of all four candidates in the party. Because of this, he knew he had to work harder than all of them combined, and he did. He bridged existing divides in the party to gain the support of the Illinois delegation. He eschewed the partisan attack language his opponents favored, opting instead for sympathy and grace. He labored over his speeches, researching the Founding Fathers' thoughts on slavery, the Constitution, and the local perspectives in each place he visited. His perseverance, humility, and dedication paid off when he unexpectedly secured the nomination and went on to become the 16th president of the United States.

THEODORE ROOSEVELT

Key Takeaway: A great tragedy altered Roosevelt's life and career.

On the evening that his very first daughter was born, at the age of twenty-six, Teddy Roosevelt suffered a loss greater than most men face in their entire lives. His mother died suddenly from Typhoid fever, and—not twelve hours later—his wife succumbed to a kidney disease that had been masked by the pregnancy. After his tragic loss, Roosevelt threw himself into his work almost too fervently. He was back at the Assembly two days later but consumed himself with a "legislative frenzy" that soon wore through the goodwill from his personal tragedy. Ready to leave the state legislature, he stayed to fight one last fight against the corrupt party bosses and their objectionable presidential candidate, James Blaine.

Roosevelt considered himself a reformist Republican and won the support of independents for vocally opposing Blaine and his corruption, going so far as to support the Democratic candidate instead. When Blaine won anyway, Roosevelt backslid, supporting the choice the party had made in Blaine. Hated by the post-Civil War Republicans for opposing Blaine and hated by the reformists and independents for his reversal, Roosevelt removed himself from political life completely.

Key Takeaway: Roosevelt retreated to the North Dakota wilderness to reinvent himself.

Purchasing a large cattle ranch in the Badlands of North Dakota, Roosevelt looked to heal the wounds of his tragic loss, both of his personal and professional life. Where Lincoln shared his grief and troubles with friends and family, Roosevelt turned inward, trying desperately to "work" the depression out of himself. He rode horses for sixteen hours a day and toughened himself with the difficult work of cattle ranching. He spoke to no one of his grief, refused to even utter his newborn daughter's name (Alice, after her mother), and burned any photos or reminders of his life with her. For Roosevelt, depression was a weakness and a sickness that needed to be ignored until it disappeared. During this time, Roosevelt wrote the most important works of his life including *Hunting Trips of a Ranchman, Ranch Life and the Hunting Trail, and The Winning of the West.*

His two years at the ranch did as intended. Not only did he heal himself of the wounds of his loss, he strengthened himself both inward and outward. He overcame a great many fears, his "nervous and timid" nature, and even overcame his own asthma. Through sheer power of will, Roosevelt returned to the East Coast a tougher, grittier man—a hybrid of Eastern and Western that forever changed the way people perceived him. Upon his return, he reconnected with a childhood friend, Edith Carow, whom he soon married. Above all, Roosevelt's tragedy reshaped the way he saw the world—rather now through luck and chance, easy to change on a whim—than a story he could write himself.

Key Takeaway: Roosevelt went on a rampage against corruption.

With his new lease on the transient nature of life, Roosevelt took two relatively unprestigious positions against the advice of his closest friends. As a member of the Civil Service Commission and a member of the New York Police Board, Roosevelt made it his personal mission to root out the rampant corruption that plagued the departments. He aimed to change the very structure of the system from one which rewarded only those with connections and money for bribes to a pure meritocracy. While many championed his fight against corruption, he was deeply unpopular with those who benefitted from the way things were. Amidst this vitriol against him, Roosevelt took a hiatus from the Police Board to stump for William McKinley. Though his fight against corruption made him deeply unpopular in New York, it made him a compelling figure on the campaign trail. Once McKinley was elected, Roosevelt was hoping for a high position in the cabinet, but due to Roosevelt's "pugnacious" nature, he was appointed instead as assistant secretary of the navy—a post he accepted against the advice of his friends once again.

Key Takeaway: Roosevelt honed his leadership through subordination and battle.

As assistant to the Secretary of the Navy, Roosevelt was in his first purely subordinate position, which he played surprisingly well. Roosevelt wanted to bolster the navy, fighting for "preparedness in peace." He took it upon himself to first win his affection and respect, assure him of his loyalty, and then proceeded to undermine his very authority. He was convinced a war could start at any moment. Luckily for Roosevelt, he was right, and the preparedness of the navy made all the difference when the USS Maine exploded in Cuban waters and the U.S. went to war with Spain in 1898.

Roosevelt's next tactical subordination came when he joined the army—once again, against the advice of his friends. Though he was offered the post of colonel of three regiments, he declined and recommended a friend instead.

He did so because he knew his friend was more experienced preparing regiments, and he was more interested in co-leading a successful team than being the leader of an unsuccessful one.

In his co-command of the Rough Riders, Teddy assumed responsibility for the health and well-being of the men. He earned their respect by proving there wasn't anything he was asking them to do that he wouldn't do himself. The men gave him both their trust and devotion because he proved he would do anything to take care of them. In a now famous scene that ended the Spanish-American War, Teddy literally led his men into battle, charging ahead of the rest of them, forcing the Spanish to retreat and taking the city of Santiago.

Theodore Roosevelt returned from battle a national hero, but he also gained a confidence, maturity, and composure that he lacked before he left. Within three months of returning, he was elected governor of New York.

Key Takeaway: Roosevelt's ascension to the presidency was an accident.

As governor, Roosevelt was a thorn in the side of the big business interests who had long been mired in shady deals with the party bosses. As Teddy aimed to put an end to these practices, the party bosses looked for a way to get rid of an incredibly popular governor. Their solution was to nominate him for the vice presidency, where he would be effectively muzzled. While technically an honor and a promotion, the position was nothing but a figurehead with no real power to wield. Roosevelt couldn't turn it down or would risk looking pretentious and ungracious. Alas, he accepted. McKinley gave him no responsibility and never sought his advice. Roosevelt was so painfully bored, he was unsure what to do with himself throughout the day. When William McKinley was assassinated in September 1901, Theodore Roosevelt became the youngest man in the White House in history.

FRANKLIN ROOSEVELT

Key Takeaway: In 1921, Franklin Roosevelt was diagnosed with Polio, beginning a seven-year convalescence.

The paralysis that accompanied the disease was at first all-encompassing. Roosevelt could neither walk nor manage his own bodily functions. With time and determination, he slowly regained many facets of mobility. He exercised his upper body incessantly so that he could maneuver a wheelchair. He was fitted with metal braces on his legs so that he could—with great effort—walk about on his own with crutches. Through this period, Franklin relied on the same interminable optimism he used when his father fell ill. No matter how bad things were, he remained bright, cheery, and optimistic even if he didn't truly feel that way on the inside.

Due to the nature of his tragedy, Franklin could not retreat into his own world like Abraham or Theodore. Instead, he was forced to create a support team to help him with his every task. Despite his handicap, his political ambitions remained, as did his hope for a full recovery. His closest friend, Louis Howe and his devoted wife Eleanor continued to keep his name in political circles while he was away. Missy LeHand, affectionately termed his "other wife," took care of his daily needs in Florida.

Interestingly, Franklin's convalescence proved to be a time of growth for those in his inner circle as well as for himself. Eleanor found her stride in politics and public speaking, and Howe devoted himself completely to Franklin's political future. Missy guided Franklin out of the depths of depression he would often be tempted to sink into. It is important to note that none of his inner circle could be considered "yes men." They were all three known for arguing with him, counseling him, and telling him the hard truths when it needed to be done.

Key Takeaway: Hot springs and an unexpected speech defined his recovery.

When asked to attend the Democratic National Convention to support Al Smith in his bid for presidency, Franklin agreed. But the long walk up to and across a stage, when he was weak and unsteady on his crutches, could have meant a blowing embarrassment and disappointment. After training for months, Roosevelt successfully crossed the stage and—though Smith did not receive the nomination—Franklin's strength, resolve, and courage came away as the political winner of the event.

After the convention, while visiting a dilapidated hotel at a natural mineral hot spring in Warm Springs, Georgia, Roosevelt was inspired to create a therapy center for his fellow "polios," as he called them. He purchased the hotel and spent more than half of his fortune restoring it, personally taking charge of every detail. While he was hoping Warm Springs would be the cure to his paralysis, it offered him a different kind of recovery instead.

The micromanagement of every detail on the property and the day-to-day interactions with his fellow Polios instilled in Roosevelt a profound humility and empathy he had never before possessed. It rid him of the air of superiority he had oft been accused of and gave him new confidence in his leadership abilities in the face of his handicap.

Key Takeaway: FDR returns to politics; the Great Depression ensues.

After four years at Warm Springs, Al Smith once again asked for Franklin's help. Smith had finally won the nomination for president and asked Roosevelt to run as governor of New York, more as a tactic to boost voter turnout than anything else. After the election, Franklin could turn over operations to the lieutenant governor and return to Warm Springs. Smith, however, lost in a Republican wave to Herbert Hoover and, FDR, once he won the governorship, chose not to relinquish it back to Smith or anyone else.

As governor, Roosevelt employed his inner circle as his eyes and ears in the state, determined not to let his physical limitations limit his knowledge of the wellbeing of his constituents. This detailed knowledge is precisely what led him to understand the depression was coming when many others thought the economy still looked rosy.

When the Great Depression enveloped New York, Roosevelt employed his trademark trial-and-error style to find solutions to the growing unrest: he was always willing to try anything and quick to discard those methods that didn't prove to be promising. What he came up with was a comprehensive relief program to provide public work and unemployment insurance, the first program of its kind in the country.

Key Takeaway: FDR's adversity led directly to his becoming president.

As the Great Depression tightened its stranglehold on the nation, President Herbert Hoover was frozen with inaction. His blind faith in individualism and the American economy meant he couldn't admit that his policy had failed. When Roosevelt challenged Hoover, he did so as a champion of the people. Roosevelt's leadership style had been dictated by his capacity to try, fail, and adjust as well as his deep and personal understanding of human struggle—both through his own experiences and the unique, human-centric way through which he saw problems and solutions. Every story to him was a personal story.

The American people needed someone who understood their hardships—and someone who was willing to try anything to fix them.

LYNDON JOHNSON

Key Takeaway: Lyndon Johnson lost his first run for a Senate seat in 1941, leading to a long, dark period in his life.

While Johnson's "personal tragedy" may seem insignificant compared with those of Lincoln and the Roosevelts, it sent him into a similar depression all the same. Johnson utterly and completely believed that if he got up earlier and worked harder than everyone else, that every victory should be his. Despite some difficulties early in the campaign, Johnson overcame and was all but guaranteed the Senate seat. But politics were still corrupt and a swath of voters "suddenly materialized" from boss-controlled counties in Texas. He had lost.

Johnson returned to his place in Congress morally and emotionally defeated. He believed his loss meant that he had lost favor with President Roosevelt. He saw himself as a failure and believed returning to Congress as such meant he no longer carried any power or sway. Abraham, Teddy, and Theodore each had the means to pursue a different life to shake them out of their depressive states. Lyndon, however, had no such respite. He was not independently wealthy and his whole life was politics. With that seemingly taken from him, he had nothing. He became angry, temperamental, and lost focus of his desire to help people and make a difference. His staff became afraid of him. The large, impersonal nature of the House meant his particular skills to read people and win them over weren't of much use. He focused solely on amassing private wealth and drifted further politically to the right, even speaking out against the New Deal. This depressive, ill, angry, mistrustful Johnson lasted for his entire seven years in Congress.

Key Takeaway: Johnson finds himself again.

When Johnson finally made it to the Senate in 1948, his political drive was unflagging. The Senate, smaller and much more susceptible to his particular brand of politicking, was a never-ending project for him to complete. He worked early mornings, late nights, and through every weekend. He learned everything about every senator, about intricacies of the process, and used that information to quickly move his way to majority party whip and then to Senate minority leader in just five years. He had a reputation for getting things done, but still continually swung unpredictably between irascible and benevolent. Johnson may have found political success once again, but the generous man who spent his meager salary buying school supplies for the impoverished schoolchildren of Cotulla, Texas was nowhere to be found.

In 1955, Johnson suffered a near-fatal heart attack. His political ambitions were once again dashed. He fell, once again, into a deep depression. He was bedridden for months and grew despondent. Everything he had worked for his entire life seemed to have slipped away in an instant. This period away from politics entirely was Johnson's turning point. For years he had breakfasts of black coffee and cigarettes, eating only as sustenance between rushed meetings and demanding his staff work the same eighteen-hour days as he did.

As if overnight, Johnson developed a newfound appreciation for life. He started eating healthy, spending more time with his family, and even eased up on his staff. When faced with death, he was forced to ask himself what his life had been for, what his purpose had been. Amassing power and wealth, he realized, were meaningless to leave behind.

Key Takeaway: A near-death experience causes an ideological shift.

The realization Lyndon Johnson came to in the hospital was one his father had taught him: that helping people was the only true, valuable purpose in life. After eschewing the New Deal and downplaying civil rights, Johnson returned to his once-progressive stance. In his speech announcing his return to the Senate, Johnson laid forth the most progressive agenda of his career calling for broad social welfare programs and forward-thinking civil rights legislation.

When he returned to the Senate, he kept his promise. Johnson wrangled the votes of western states, mountain states, northern states, and southern states to support his

Civil Rights Act. While the final bill was somewhat watered down, and the northerners even called it weak, Johnson understood that the passage of the bill alone was enough to mark a turning point for civil rights legislation. So successful was this compromise for the party and for his career, many believed it earned him the nomination for president. However, as FDR predicted more than twenty years prior, the country wasn't ready for a southern president.

Johnson was instead on the ticket under JFK, believing he could empower the somewhat meaningless role of vice president the way he had done as senate majority whip. He was mistaken and found himself as restless and void of meaning in the vice presidency as Theodore Roosevelt had been. LBJ gave up on trying to empower the office or effect legislation and resigned himself to unfulfilling work on several committees. Until John F. Kennedy, like William McKinley, was assassinated, hurling LBJ suddenly into power.

PART III: HOW THEY LED

TRANSFORMATIONAL LEADERSHIP

Though Lincoln vehemently opposed slavery, he believed so thoroughly in the power of the Constitution and the rights of the states that he wouldn't dare issue a unilateral proclamation ordering its abolition as president. As the Civil War raged on however, he came to the conclusion that slavery was the only reason the South was winning, and thus, slavery was a direct threat to the sanctity of the Union. As the President, it was within Lincoln's powers of war to put an end to any threat to the Union or the Constitution. This technical loophole is what gave Lincoln the confidence in his justification of the Emancipation Proclamation.

Despite the decree being a unilateral decision on Lincoln's part, however, he viewed it as a last resort. He had presented every other option to the Senate, to Congress, to the states, and to his cabinet. He knew that slavery was wrong, and it must end, but he made it clear that, if necessary, he would take unilateral action.

Even when he finally came to this decision, he toiled over every possible objection. He carefully ran through the arguments he knew each of his cabinet members would make for or against it and prepared his own measured responses to those questions. When the time came, he dutifully deliberated once again on every objection or consideration they raised, and gave them all a chance to publicly object and absolve themselves of any credit for it. Knowing how politically dangerous this was, he was more than willing to take full responsibility for the weight of his actions.

Because Lincoln had staffed his cabinet with members from each of the disparate factions around the nation, disagreement was rife. But Abraham had a unique way of understanding what each man needed and fostering respectful debate over petty squabbles. He made everyone feel intimately respected, and never let personal feelings interfere with his decisions. Edwin Stanton, Lincoln's secretary of war during this crucial period, had humiliated and shunned the "prairie lawyer" Lincoln in his youth. As president, however, Lincoln recognized he was the best man for the job and put his past embarrassment aside. When Lincoln was angry, he would write a letter to the receiving party and then promptly file it away, never to be sent.

Once the Emancipation Proclamation was issued, there was another 100 days until it would go into action. Lincoln hoped in this time the South would surrender. They did not. The Union lost ground, the Republicans had lost ground in the mid-term elections, and morale was at an all-time low, both for the troops and for Lincoln himself. Despite this, he persevered in positivity wherever he could.

When it came time to sign the Proclamation, many tried to convince Lincoln to walk it back, to save abolition for another day, and work instead toward mending the Union. But Lincoln, above all, was a man of his word. Despite the risks and the wave of anti-abolition sentiment, Lincoln believed wholeheartedly that what he was doing was the right thing, and that the people would come around. He listened carefully to the changing sentiments in the months since he first made the decree public. He understood that, though it may not seem so, the public was slowly changing its mind. When he signed the Emancipation Proclamation freeing the slaves on January 1, 1863 he had no doubt in his mind that he had made the right choice.

The country however, lagged slightly behind. While people celebrated in Massachusetts, many soldiers were "fighting for the Union, not emancipation" and many of the border states threatened to join the Confederacy. Lincoln had predicted this, but also believed that the spirit of emancipation would swell in them and call them to a higher purpose.

Goodwin focuses intently on Lincoln's ability as a transformational versus a transactional leader. Lincoln didn't just make deals or offer incentives or *quid pro quos*—though he certainly did use these tools to his advantage—he inspired people to action on a cause greater than themselves. The sacrifice he asked of the soldiers was for a higher moral purpose: the freedom of all men. Though only three of ten soldiers were willing to fight for emancipation in the first eighteen months of the war, that number grew to a vast majority after the Proclamation was signed. This transformation, of course, didn't happen overnight. It happened because Lincoln made himself accessible to the soldiers at the heart of the cause. The names "Uncle Abe" and "Father Abraham" came into being because those soldiers genuinely believed in the convictions of the man who had asked them to fight. Lincoln visited camps, answered individual letters, and showed genuine compassion, empathy, kindness, and responsibility for each and every soldier. Those men were happy to die for the cause because they understood that the war weighed as heavily on him as it did on them, that the cause was so important that Lincoln would sacrifice running for another term before walking back any part of what they were fighting for.

Lincoln may have died before the Emancipation Proclamation was fully ratified, but, as Goodwin notes, the social transformation he shepherded would draw a line in United States history, before and after Abraham Lincoln.

Abraham Lincoln's Key Leadership Skills

Goodwin summarized Lincoln's leadership skills as follows:

- *Acknowledge when failed policies demand a change in direction (p. 213).*
- *Gather firsthand information, ask questions (p. 214).*
- *Find time and space in which to think (p. 214).*
- *Exhaust all possibility of compromise before exercising unilateral power (p. 215).*
- *Anticipate contending viewpoints (p. 218).*
- *Assume full responsibility for a pivotal decision (p. 220)*
- *Understand the emotional needs of each member of the team (p. 223).*

- *Refuse to let past resentments fester; transcend personal vendettas (p. 224).*

- *Set a standard of mutual respect and dignity; control anger (p. 225)*

- *Shield colleagues from blame (p. 226).*

- *Maintain perspective in the face of both accolades and abuse (pp. 226–227).*

- *Find ways to cope with pressure, maintain balance, replenish energy (p. 227).*

- *Keep your word (p. 230).*

- *Know when to hold back, when to move forward (p. 232).*

- *Combine transactional and transformational leadership (p. 234)*

- *Be accessible, easy to approach (p. 235).*

- *Put ambition for the collective interest above self-interest (p. 238).*

CRISIS MANAGEMENT

Goodwin devotes the section on Theodore Roosevelt's presidential leadership to his handling of the Great Coal Strike of 1902. Coal miners, frustrated with 10-hour days, brutal working conditions, and low wages went on strike against what had become the largest conglomerate of coal operators in history. With the operators unwilling to concede on any front, nor even recognize the legitimacy of the union, the strike would go on for six months—and change the face of the presidency—before the coal miners finally went back to work.

At the time, it was unheard of for a president to intervene in what were considered private matters between labor and owner, but Roosevelt saw the Great Coal Strike for what it was: a potentially dangerous situation that could harm millions of Americans if coal production didn't resume before winter. He knew he had to act, but also knew he had no legal right to do so, and that moving forward too swiftly could be seen as a gross abuse and expansion of presidential power. Not a man for passivity, however, he moved forward slowly, laying the groundwork for executive action to avoid a state of emergency. Roosevelt saw himself ultimately as the protector of the people, and if a dispute between owner and laborer were to bring harm to the general public, then it was absolutely within his purview to take action.

He first commissioned an independent report on the state of the situation but decided not to publish it in order to avoid being committed so soon to a single course of action. When violence erupted outside of one of the mines, killing several miners, Roosevelt avoided taking sides and let the president of the miners ease the tensions. His patience and silence proved to be another wise maneuver. As tensions escalated, Roosevelt reevaluated his decision to withhold the report, now believing it was in the interest of the people to release it. Though met with derision from many reporters about his getting involved in affairs in which he had no business, ultimately, he was preparing his place as a necessary piece of this conflict.

In order to garner the support of the people, Roosevelt went on a "barnstorming" speaking tour to those most affected by the crisis. Though he avoided speaking directly about the strike in his speeches, he championed a "a square deal for every man, great or small, rich or poor." He believed it was time for public sentiment to move forward to allow government to regulate trusts and address growing inequality.

With broad support by those most affected, and increasing reports of the damage the strike was already creating, Roosevelt chose to take action. He assembled a team of diverse opinion and expertise to help advise him, and he convened a meeting between the coal owners and union representatives on neutral ground in Washington D.C. While both Roosevelt and John Mitchell, the president of the labor union, were reasonable, calm, and willing to negotiate, the coal barons were rude, obtuse, uncompromising and entitled. When a transcript of the meeting (the first of its kind to be recorded) was released to the papers, public opinion overwhelmingly swayed in favor of the strikers.

The meeting had failed, but Teddy refused to "sit supinely by." He was prepared, like Lincoln was, to resort to the most drastic action if necessary, but was also ready to try any less egregious options to avoid it. Trying to bring compromise failed again, and Roosevelt turned to his last resort: he threatened the full force of the United States Army against the operators and would divest them of their property if they did not comply.

"Don't hit unless you have to, but when you hit, hit hard." (p. 266).

Like Lincoln, Roosevelt welcomed his cabinet to oppose him and absolve themselves of any responsibility. He was fully and solely accountable for the choices he was making. Luckily, it didn't have to come to that. Roosevelt's secretary of war, Elihu Root, volunteered to visit with the coal barons as a "private citizen" to help broker a deal that wouldn't involve John Mitchell, whom the coal owners refused to negotiate with.

The plan was successful—though it was the same exact plan Mitchell first suggested—and a presidential commission was formed to assess the situation and provide a recommended solution. Both parties would agree to abide by the third-party decision. As it was, the miners went back to work with shorter workdays and a 10 percent raise. Roosevelt, upon this victory for the American people, was quick to share the praise with everyone on the team he had assembled. Soon thereafter, he made a point to document the entire course of his decision-making process from the very beginning, such that future administrations might come to understand how this presidential power of supervision and regulation was granted.

Theodore Roosevelt's Key Leadership Skills

- *Calculate risks of getting involved (p. 247)*
- *Secure a reliable understanding of the facts, causes, and conditions of the situation (p.248)*

- Remain uncommitted in the early stages (p. 249)

- Use history to provide perspective (p 250).

- Be ready to grapple with reversals, abrupt intrusions that can unravel all plans (p.252).

- Reevaluate options; be ready to adapt as a situation escalates (p. 253).

- Be visible. Cultivate public support among those most directly affected by the crisis (p. 255).

- Clear the deck to focus with single-mindedness on the crisis (p 256).

- Assemble a crisis management team (p 258).

- Frame the narrative (p. 260).

- Keep temper in check (p 261).

- Document proceedings each step of the way (p. 262).

- Control the message in the press (p. 263).

- Find ways to relieve stress (p. 264).

- Be ready with multiple strategies; prepare contingent moves (p. 266).

- Don't hit unless you have to, but when you hit, hit hard (p. 266).

- Find ways to save face (p. 268).

- Share credit for the successful resolution (p. 270).

- Leave a record behind for the future (p. 271).

TURNAROUND LEADERSHIP

When Franklin Delano Roosevelt took office in 1932, the country was deep in the throes of the Great Depression, and the American people were desperate for change. Banks, which had invested people's savings into speculative stocks, lost everything when the market crashed and were unable to cover withdrawals. The more banks became insolvent, the more people panicked and tried to withdraw their money for fear it would be lost forever, and the more banks started shutting their doors. People lost their life savings, their homes, their farms, their jobs, and their faith in the American economic system. Unemployment was at 25 percent and a dark cloud hung over the nation. Many believed the American experiment was over and the country would never recover.

FDR knew before he was even sworn in that decisive action was a must. He knew that to restore confidence in the American people he must immediately draw a line before and after—to let the people know that things would be different going forward. In his inauguration, Roosevelt was the first president to repeat the entire oath, word for word, instead of just responding, *I do*. His inauguration speech is when he famously uttered, "the only thing we have to fear is fear itself." President Hoover had been unable to address his own failings and unwilling to admit how bad things had gotten. But FDR understood the need to embrace the gravity of the situation in order to move forward.

The day Roosevelt took office, he moved swiftly to find precedent for a president to gain sweeping authority over the financial system. He needed to close the banks and restructure them while restoring confidence in the American people. In a country that had believed firmly in laissez-faire economics, never would there be a greater shift of the balance of power between government and industry. He got the banks closed and had exactly one week to fix them and reopen them. He jammed legislation quickly through a strongly Democratic Senate and House, but with the full support of Republicans who appreciated the importance of swift action.

Roosevelt's personal struggles—his battle with Polio; his ability to face any situation with optimism; his experience building, running, and personally managing the Warm Springs treatment center   gave him a unique set of skills to manage the Great Depression from a personal, human perspective. He knew the people needed to hear that they weren't to blame; they needed to understand the problem and be able to envision the solution. In order to speak directly to the nation, Roosevelt began the intimate "Fireside Chats" he was famed for. His warmth and confidence in that first chat, the night before the banks reopened, reinstilled American confidence in the banking system. The next morning, people were lining up to put their money back into the banks.

Unlike Abraham and his older cousin Teddy, Franklin stocked his cabinet with trusted colleagues who would let him lead, not challenge his every decision. He needed people who were willing to innovate, to take chances, but who were also ready to fail. Franklin asked Congress to stay for an emergency 100-day session to pass as much legislation as possible, noting that the emergency banking bill was a band-aid, not a cure to the systemic ailment that had caused the collapse. In those 100 days, fifteen major bills were passed, billions of dollars appropriated to "undertake massive public works, provide direct work relief, ease mortgage distress, safeguard investors, guarantee bank deposits, ensure decent wages, provide collective bargaining, raise agricultural prices, generate public power" (Goodwin, p. 293).

People were amazed at how much he was able to get done because he was willing to work ceaselessly and to try anything. New agencies fostering a culture of innovation were created to replace the stale, bureaucratic status quo. In his first eighteen months, he created twenty such "alphabet soup" agencies including the CCC, PWA, FDIC, TVA, FHA, FCC, SEC, WPA, CWA, and the FSRC—many of which are still around today.

Roosevelt encouraged those beneath him to be creative, decisive, to try anything, and didn't punish those who failed. If a program wasn't working, they scrapped it and moved on. Roosevelt wasn't just fixing the symptoms of the depression, but was effecting systemic change in a system he saw as harmful to the very people who trusted in it. With all the change he was enacting, Roosevelt was always sure to communicate with the people, forging an unprecedented relationship to the press to uphold the trust and confidence of the country. It was a period of unparalleled cooperation in government. Perhaps only a man with the particular character, optimism, and communication skills of FDR could have steered the nation back on course.

Franklin Roosevelt's Key Leadership Skills

- *Draw an immediate sharp line of demarcation between what has gone before and what is about to begin (p. 276).*

- *Restore confidence to the spirit and morale of the people. Strike the right balance of realism and optimism (p. 277).*

- *Infuse a sense of shared purpose and direction (p. 278).*

- *Tell people what they can expect and what is expected of them (p. 279).*

- *Lead by example (p. 280)*

- *Forge a team aligned with action and change (p 281).*

- *Create a gathering pause, a window of time (p. 282).*

- *Bring all stakeholders aboard (p. 283).*

- *Set a deadline and drive full-bore to meet it (p. 284).*

- *Set forth and maintain clear-cut ground rules with the press (p. 287).*

- *Tell the story simply, directly to the people (p. 289).*

- *Address systemic problems. Launch lasting reforms (p. 291).*

- *Be open to experiment. Design flexible agencies to deal with new problems (p. 293).*

- *Stimulate competition and debate. Encourage creativity (p. 296).*

- *Open channels of unfiltered information to supplement and challenge official sources (p. 300).*

- *Adapt. Be ready to change course quickly when necessary (p. 301).*

VISIONARY LEADERSHIP

When President Kennedy was assassinated in November 1963, Lyndon Johnson knew that his first actions as president had to be swift, decisive, and compassionate. He saw the great possibility to use the sympathy of the American people to propel Kennedy's own agenda after his death. He vowed to pass Kennedy's tax cut and civil rights act without delay. In his very first speech to the American people the day after Kennedy was shot, he won over the country with his solemnity, his purpose, and his vision of Congress overcoming the deep divides that had plagued them for years.

Johnson knew that he had to simplify the agenda in order to capitalize on the national mood. A procedural genius, he worked feverishly to get Kennedy's tax cut and civil rights bill pushed through a government that had been deadlocked since Kennedy took office. One of his greatest skills was knowing each Senator, what they were like, what they needed to hear, and expertly negotiating for their support. When Johnson promised a Senator something in return for his support, he lived up to that promise. When transactional leadership wasn't enough to sway a conservative senator from Illinois to support a civil rights bill deeply unpopular with Republicans, he appealed to his own ego and desire to make his mark on history—he called to the "party of Lincoln" to make the right choice. He was a master of the personal relationships needed to push government forward.

When Johnson got his tax cut and passed the sweeping Civil Rights Act of 1964, it was time to move into his own vision for America: The Great Society. Johnson received his mandate for president when he won his election in a landslide against Barry Goldwater. Now was the time to expand voting rights, Medicare, education spending, and other social welfare programs to help the elderly and the poor. His father imbued in him the belief that the purpose of government was to uplift every citizen and give them the opportunity to succeed—the same belief that he shared with FDR, and one that echoed Lincoln as well.

To that end, Johnson put all of his political capital on the line to achieve his goals. He called in every favor, worked tirelessly, played the system he knew so well, and the 89th Congress passed a dizzying number of laws during its historic session. But Johnson also knew when to hold back, and he sensed the timing wasn't yet right for the voting rights act. In 1966, in the midst of Bloody Sunday and marches in Selma and around the country, Lyndon called leaders of Congress to a special session at the White House. It was there he made an impassioned speech, calling for all to rise above the history of violence and discrimination, to rise above Democrat or Republican, to rise above Northern or Southern, to see that the issue of negro voting rights was an issue of *human* rights. Just 623 days after Kennedy's assassination, the Voting Rights Act was passed—Johnson had accomplished everything he set out to do as president in under two years.

Lyndon Johnson's Key Leadership Skills

- *Make a dramatic start (p. 309).*

- *Lead with your strengths (p. 309).*

- *Simplify the agenda (p. 311).*

- *Establish the most effective order of battle (p. 312).*

- *Honor commitments (p. 314).*

- *Drive, drive, drive (p. 315).*

- *Master the power of narrative (p. 316).*

- *Know for what and when to risk it all (p. 318).*

- *Rally support around a strategic target (p. 318).*

- *Draw a clear line of battle (p. 321).*

- *Impose discipline in the ranks (p. 322).*

- *Identify the key to success. Put ego aside (p. 323).*

- *Take the measure of the man (p. 324).*

- *Set forth a compelling picture of the future (p. 326).*

- *The readiness is all (p. 327).*

- *Give stakeholders a chance to shape measures from the start (p. 329).*

- *Know when to hold back, when to move forward (p. 331).*

- *Let celebrations honor the past and provide momentum for the future p. 335).*

On Vietnam

All the decisiveness and vision that Johnson had in his domestic policy he lacked in his foreign policy. He may have inherited the war in Vietnam, but no historian will argue he handled it well. He capitulated on most decisions to a limited team of advisors—who consistently advocated to increase troops—and tried his best to hide the decisions he was making from the American people for fear it could become a roadblock to his Great Society initiatives passing in Congress. But the people of a nation can only get behind a war if they believe in what they are fighting for and if they believe in the very institutions they are protecting. That sense of shared direction and purpose that propelled the U.S. in World War II was missing in Vietnam, the American public felt outraged and lied to, and Johnson withdrew his name from reelection in 1968. As Goodwin notes:

"The fault line through Lyndon Johnson's presidency would split his legacy and haunt him for the rest of his life." (Goodwin, p. 343)

EPILOGUE

In the epilogue, entitled "Of Death and Remembrance," Goodwin opines on the time she spent with LBJ near the end of his life helping him to write his memoirs on his ranch in Texas. He was ashamed of Vietnam, considered it his biggest failure, and wanted more to be remembered for his work on civil rights. After Johnson stepped down from politics in a wave of public disapproval, he knew his time was up and his political capital had been spent. He spent the last years of his life likely wishing there was more he could do and regretting that writing a memoir meant his time of action had come to an end.

For Theodore, the end of his time as president was similarly disquieting. Giving up his chance at a third term in order to respect the unwritten rule of term limits, he regretted the decision before the election was even held. Alas, he was a man of his word. He left office in 1908 but attempted to run again in 1912, losing the nomination to the very man he had chosen to succeed him, William Howard Taft. For years after he remained heavily involved in the political sphere, ever contemplating running again, and never finding the right time before his unexpected death in 1919 at the age of sixty.

Franklin Roosevelt's life was oft defined by avoiding the very appearance of illness—from pretending he wasn't sick to protect his ailing father to projecting an endlessly optimistic façade in his long struggle with Polio. The same was true of the acute congested heart failure that plagued him in his final years. Despite this, the ever-resilient man carried gingerly on, hiding his illness, and winning a fourth term in the midst of World War II—the only president to serve four terms. FDR died 82 days into his fourth term, fighting for what he believed in, saving democracy, "laying the groundwork for global peace." FDR's meticulous collection of presidential letters and papers would mark the beginning of presidential libraries. His intimate brand of leadership, his connection to the American people, meant his death took a personal toll on the country he led.

The day Abraham Lincoln was shot was a happy day for him. The war was ending, the Confederate Capitol at Richmond had been evacuated, and he was making plans for the reconstruction of the country he so dearly loved. John Wilkes Booth believed Lincoln was a tyrant and that he would go down in history as a hero for killing him. Instead, Lincoln has gone down in history as one of the greatest leaders this country has ever known. Goodwin closes the book reflecting on the impact Lincoln's leadership has had on future American leaders—his belief in the importance of education, of remembering the history and foundation of this great country in order to understand its future path. Lincoln's empathy, humility, purpose, and wisdom have thus served as a moral compass for the American people for centuries since his death and likely will for centuries to come.

EDITORIAL REVIEW

Leadership in Turbulent Times is a masterpiece of detailed presidential history and a thorough examination of what makes a leader, and what made each of these four presidents particularly significant. Goodwin addresses the roots of leadership, asks whether leaders are born or made, and asks whether the leader makes the times, or the times make the leader. Ultimately, there is no one set path to leadership, but resilience, determination, and a sense of moral purpose were something they all shared.

The stories Goodwin relays are almost painfully detailed with minute-by-minute descriptions of meetings, letters, and personal conversations. While she spent significant time working with LBJ, her stories of the previous presidents do not suffer in detail by comparison. Rather than an overarching review of their presidencies, she focuses on their early personal lives and their actions throughout a single presidential issue. For Lincoln, it was the seminal and fraught decision to move forward with the Emancipation Proclamation. For Teddy Roosevelt it was his deft handling of the Great Coal Strike of 1902. For FDR, of course, it was his turnaround of the country in the hopelessness of the Great Depression. Though many would argue that Lyndon Johnson doesn't belong on this list due to his soiled legacy of the Vietnam War, the leadership he showed in the Great Society and his unmatched legislative prowess paint a unique type of leader pushing the country into civil rights victories despite strong resistance from southern states.

Each of the men had a different leadership style; they each faced a different tragedy and dealt with those tragedies in different ways. Each man had a different childhood, and a different temperament—where Abraham was gregarious, Theodore was timid; where Lyndon was a tough Texas kid, Franklin enjoyed a wealthy and oft spoiled childhood—but they all had one thing in common: they were all the perfect leaders to come in at their perfect time in America's history.

Goodwin notes that each of the four leaders as well found an idol in the one before him. Teddy Roosevelt greatly looked up to Lincoln and found strength and resolve in reading his ten-volume biography. Theodore was a mentor to his younger cousin Franklin, and Lyndon Johnson believed his Great Society was the natural continuation of FDR's New Deal that lifted America out of the Great Depression.

They also had one more thing in common: they believed in the greatness of this nation and in the idea that the government wasn't just there to make laws, but to enrich and support the lives of the people. Each of these four men were guided by a strong moral compass and unflagging determination, and they each unquestionably enriched the lives of the Americans they led.

BACKGROUND ON AUTHOR

Doris Helen Kearns Goodwin is an American biographer, historian, and political commentator. She has written several presidential biographies and her book *No Ordinary Time: Franklin and Eleanor Roosevelt: The Home Front in World War II* won the Pulitzer Prize for History in 1995. Goodwin attended Colby College in Maine where she received Bachelor of Arts and graduated *magna cum laude*. In 1964, she received the Woodrow Wilson fellowship and pursued her doctoral studies at Harvard.

Goodwin worked closely with Lyndon B. Johnson as a White House Fellow in the 60s and helped him complete his memoirs, *Lyndon Johnson and the American Dream*. After leaving the White House, she taught government at Harvard for more than ten years. Her book *Team of Rivals: The Political Genius of Abraham Lincoln* won the 2005 Lincoln Prize for the best book about the American Civil War and was also the basis for the feature film, *Lincoln*.

Goodwin is a regular political commentator and has appeared on *Meet the Press*, *Charlie Rose*, and NBC News, among others.

TITLES BY DORIS KEARNS GOODWIN

Lyndon Johnson and the American Dream. 1977.

The Fitzgeralds and the Kennedys: An American Saga. 1987.

No Ordinary Time: Franklin and Eleanor Roosevelt: The Home Front in World War II. 1994.

Wait Till Next Year: A Memoir. 1997.

Every Four Years: Presidential Campaign Coverage from 1896 to 2000. 2000.

Team of Rivals: The Political Genius of Abraham Lincoln. 2005.

The Bully Pulpit: Theodore Roosevelt, William Howard Taft, and the Golden Age of Journalism. 2013.

Leadership in Turbulent Times. 2018.

If you enjoyed this ZIP Reads publication, we encourage you to purchase a copy of <u>the original book.</u>

We'd also love an honest review on Amazon.com!

Want **FREE** book summaries delivered weekly? Sign up for our email list and get notified of all our new releases, free promos, and $0.99 deals!

No spam, just books.

Sign up at **<u>http://zipreads.co</u>**